foreword

A glass of wine has a well-established place on the table alongside your dinner, but what about in the meal itself? Wine can add a whole new level of flavour to your favourite dishes, and it works wonders in a marinade.

Cooking with wine is effortless as long as you keep a few things in mind. First, never cook with a wine you wouldn't drink. As wine cooks, the alcohol evaporates and the flavour and acidity become concentrated. If you don't like the taste of the wine in your glass, you won't like the more pronounced flavour in your dish. Similarly, less is more. Add too much wine and as its flavours become concentrated, it will completely overpower the dish. Finally, pair the right wine with the right dish. As a general rule, red wines are best with dark meats and white wines are best with white or light meats though both are fine for pork. Full-bodied wines work better in hearty or highly seasoned dishes, whereas dry, light wines are more suited to light, creamy dishes.

So grab your corkscrew, flip through the recipes that follow, and get ready to create some culinary magic cooking with wine!

Jean Paré

Chicken Marsala

This casually elegant dish combines tender chicken with mushrooms and Marsala wine. It goes great with buttered noodles with herbs.

Butter	1 tbsp.	15 mL
Boneless, skinless chicken breast halves (about 5 oz., 140 g, each)	4	4
Salt, to taste		
Pepper, to taste		
Sliced fresh white mushrooms	2 cups	500 mL
Prepared chicken broth	3/4 cup	175 mL
Marsala wine	1/2 cup	125 mL
Water	1 tbsp.	15 mL
Cornstarch	2 tsp.	10 mL
Chopped fresh chives	1 tbsp.	15 mL

Melt butter in a large frying pan on medium-high. Sprinkle chicken with salt and pepper. Cook until all sides of chicken are browned. Transfer to a large plate.

Add mushrooms to same frying pan. Cook for about 5 minutes, stirring occasionally, until mushrooms are softened and liquid is evaporated. Stir in broth and wine and bring to a boil.

Stir water into cornstarch in a small cup until smooth. Add to mushroom mixture. Cook, stirring, until boiling and thickened. Add chicken. Reduce heat to medium-low and simmer, covered, for about 5 minutes, turning chicken occasionally, until heated through. Sprinkle with chives. Makes 4 servings.

1 serving: 240 Calories; 4.5 g Total Fat (1 g Mono, 0.5 g Poly, 2.5 g Sat); 90 mg Cholesterol; 7 g Carbohydrate (0 g Fibre, 3 g Sugar); 33 g Protein; 220 mg Sodium

Chicken Cacciatore

Wine and capers add loads of flavour to this saucy dish that is perfect for serving over pasta or rice.

Olive oil	1 tbsp.	15 mL
Boneless, skinless chicken thighs, quartered	1 1/2 lbs.	680 g
Sliced fresh white mushrooms	2 cups	500 mL
Chopped onion	1 cup	250 mL
Garlic cloves, minced	2	2
Dry white wine	1/2 cup	125 mL
Can of diced tomatoes (28 oz., 796 mL), with juice	1	1
Chopped red pepper	1 1/2 cups	375 mL
Chopped sun-dried tomatoes in oil	1/4 cup	60 mL
Tomato paste (see Tip, page 64)	3 tbsp.	45 mL
Capers	2 tbsp.	30 mL
Dried basil	1 tsp.	5 mL
Dried oregano	1 tsp.	5 mL
Granulated sugar	1 tsp.	5 mL
Bay leaf	1	1
Salt	1/2 tsp.	2 mL
Pepper	1/4 tsp.	1 mL

Heat olive oil in a large saucepan on medium-high. Add chicken. Cook for about 10 minutes, turning occasionally, until chicken starts to brown. Reduce heat to medium.

Add next 3 ingredients. Cook for about 8 minutes, stirring often, until onion is softened.

Add wine. Cook for 2 minutes, scraping any brown bits from bottom of pan.

Stir in remaining 11 ingredients. Bring to a boil, then reduce heat to medium-low. Simmer, partially covered, for 25 minutes to blend flavours. Discard bay leaf. Makes about 7 cups (1.75 L).

1 cup (250 mL): *190 Calories; 6 g Total Fat (2.5 g Mono, 1 g Poly, 1.5 g Sat); 80 mg Cholesterol; 11 g Carbohydrate (2 g Fibre, 7 g Sugar); 21 g Protein; 700 mg Sodium*

Coq au Vin

While many people think of Coq au Vin as a dish using red wine, it is actually meant to be a dish using the "local" wine, so many regions of France have variations of the dish—even Coq au Champagne! Serve over hot buttered noodles.

Unsalted butter	2 tbsp.	30 mL
Bacon, diced	2/3 cup	150 mL
Free-range chicken, cut into 8 pieces (3 to 4 lbs., 1.5 to 2 kg)	1	1
Salt, to taste		
Pepper, to taste		
Medium onions, chopped	2	2
Carrot, chopped	1	1
Celery root, diced	1 cup	250 mL
Garlic cloves, sliced	2	2
All-purpose flour	2 tbsp.	30 mL
Pinot Noir	3 cups	750 mL
Sprigs of fresh thyme	4	4
Prepared chicken broth	8 cups	2 L
Unsalted butter	1/4 cup	60 mL
Small whole white button mushrooms	2 cups	500 mL
Salt, to taste		
Pepper, to taste		

Melt first amount of butter in a heavy-bottomed casserole. Add bacon and cook on medium heat until crisp. Drain on paper towels and place in a large bowl.

Season chicken with salt and pepper and cook in bacon drippings until golden brown. Transfer to bowl with bacon.

Add onions, carrot and celery root to pan and cook on medium, stirring occasionally, until onion is translucent. Add garlic, then stir in flour and cook for 3 to 5 minutes.

Add chicken, bacon, wine, thyme and enough chicken broth to cover chicken. Bring to a boil, reduce heat and cook, partially covered, for 45 minutes to 1 hour until chicken is tender.

Meanwhile, melt remaining butter in a small pan and sauté mushrooms until golden. Season lightly with salt and pepper, then add to chicken. Ladle some sauce into a saucepan and reduce on high heat until thick and glossy. Makes 6 servings.

1 serving: *970 Calories; 38 g Total Fat (14 g Mono, 4.5 g Poly, 16 g Sat); 280 mg Cholesterol; 19 g Carbohydrate (1 g Fibre, 5 g Sugar); 88 g Protein; 1340 mg Sodium*

Phyllo-wrapped Chicken with Port Wine Sauce

Stuffed chicken breasts wrapped in phyllo and topped with a beautiful sauce—the layers of this dish add up to perfection.

Cooking oil	1 tsp.	5 mL
Thinly sliced leek (white part only)	1 cup	250 mL
Garlic cloves, minced	2	2
Grated orange zest	1 tsp.	5 mL
Pepper	1/4 tsp.	1 mL
Boneless, skinless chicken breast halves (about 5 oz., 140 g, each)	4	4
Frozen phyllo pastry sheets, thawed according to package directions	8	8
Prepared chicken broth	1 tbsp.	15 mL
Diced onion	1/2 cup	125 mL
Port	1/2 cup	125 mL
Prepared chicken broth	1/2 cup	125 mL
Redcurrant jelly	3 tbsp.	15 mL

Heat cooking oil in a medium frying pan on medium-low. Add leek and garlic, and cook for about 10 minutes, stirring occasionally, until leek is softened. Stir in orange zest and pepper.

Cut a deep pocket into side of each chicken breast, almost through to the other side. Fill with leek mixture and press to seal openings.

Lay 1 pastry sheet on waxed paper on counter. Lightly spray pastry sheet with cooking spray. Repeat with 2 more sheets. Cover remaining sheets with a damp tea towel. Cut pastry in half crosswise. Place 1 chicken breast 1 inch (2.5 cm) from short end and roll to enclose. Place seam side down on a lightly greased baking sheet with sides. Repeat with remaining pastry and chicken. Spray lightly with cooking spray and bake in 400°F (200°C) oven for about 15 minutes until pastry is browned.

For the sauce, heat first amount of broth in a medium frying pan on medium. Add onion and cook for 5 minutes, until softened. Add remaining 3 ingredients and stir until jelly melts. Boil, uncovered, on medium-high for about 10 minutes until thickened. Serve with chicken parcels. Makes 4 servings.

1 serving: *400 Calories; 3.5 g Total Fat (1 g Mono, 0.5 g Poly, 1.5 g Sat); 65 mg Cholesterol; 48 g Carbohydrate (3 g Fibre, 14 g Sugar); 34 g Protein; 420 mg Sodium*

Raspberry Chicken

Sweet yet tangy, this dish is a sure winner! Remember to allow plenty of time for the chicken to properly marinate.

Raspberry jam	1 cup	250 mL
Dry white wine	2/3 cup	150 mL
Raspberry red wine vinegar	1/2 cup	125 mL
Soy sauce	2 tbsp.	30 mL
Dijon mustard	2 tsp.	10 mL
Garlic cloves, minced	2	2
Chicken legs, back attached (about 11 oz., 310 g, each), skin removed	8	8
Water	1/4 cup	60 mL
Cornstarch	2 tbsp.	30 mL
Chopped fresh parsley, for garnish		

Combine first 6 ingredients in small bowl. Transfer to a large resealable freezer bag.

Add chicken. Turn until coated. Let stand, covered, in refrigerator for at least 4 hours or overnight, turning occasionally. Transfer chicken with raspberry mixture to a 4 to 5 quart (4 to 5 L) slow cooker. Cook, covered, on Low for 8 to 9 hours or on High for 4 to 4 1/2 hours. Transfer chicken to a serving dish using a slotted spoon. Skim and discard fat from surface of liquid in slow cooker.

Stir water into cornstarch in a small cup. Stir into liquid in slow cooker and cook, covered, on High for about 5 minutes until boiling and thickened. Pour over chicken. Garnish with parsley. Makes 8 servings.

1 serving: 520 Calories; 16 g Total Fat (4.5 g Mono, 4 g Poly, 4 g Sat); 250 mg Cholesterol; 29 g Carbohydrate (0 g Fibre, 24 g Sugar); 60 g Protein; 530 mg Sodium

Easy Chicken Cassoulet

Traditionally a cassoulet takes almost 3 days to make and contains duck or goose that has been cooked in fat. This version takes a fraction of time, uses chicken and canned beans and is considerably lower in fat.

Olive oil	1 tbsp.	15 mL
Skinless, bone-in chicken thighs	12	12
Italian sausages	4	4
Bacon slices	6	6
Olive oil	1 tbsp.	15 mL
Chopped onion	2 cups	500 mL
Garlic cloves, minced	4	4
Cans of white kidney beans, rinsed and drained (19 oz., 540 mL, each)	2	2
Prepared chicken broth	2 cups	500 mL
White wine	1 cup	250 mL
Tomato paste (see Tip, page 64)	1/4 cup	60 mL
Chopped fresh thyme	1 tbsp.	15 mL
Fine fresh bread crumbs	1 1/2 cups	375 mL

Heat first amount of olive oil in a large pot on medium-high. Sear chicken, in 2 batches, for about 10 minutes until browned. Remove from pot. Add sausages and cook for about 10 minutes until browned. Remove from pot and cut into 1 inch (2.5 cm) pieces. Reduce heat to medium and add bacon, cooking until golden. Remove and chop slices. Drain fat from pot.

Heat second amount of olive oil in same pot on medium. Add onion and cook, stirring often, for about 10 minutes until softened. Add garlic and cook for about 2 minutes until fragrant. Stir in next 5 ingredients, chicken, sausage and bacon. Cover and bring to a boil. Transfer to a greased casserole and cook, covered, in 350°F (175°C) oven for about 1 1/2 hours until sauce is thickened and chicken is tender.

Sprinkle with bread crumbs and cook, uncovered, for about 30 minutes until crumbs are golden and crisp. Makes 8 servings.

1 serving: 630 Calories; 29 g Total Fat (13 g Mono, 4.5 g Poly, 9 g Sat); 115 mg Cholesterol; 45 g Carbohydrate (13 g Fibre, 5 g Sugar); 40 g Protein; 1060 mg Sodium

Grilled Beef Tenderloin with Sautéed Chanterelles

Simple, delicious and quick to the table, this dish is the perfect late summer dinner. Look for chanterelles at your local farmers' market or specialty food store.

Beef tenderloin medallions (6 oz., 170 g, each)	4	4
Olive oil	1 tbsp.	15 mL
Shallots, sliced	3	3
Fresh chanterelles	1 lb.	454 g
Garlic clove, minced	1	1
White wine	1/2 cup	125 mL
Parsley, chopped	1 cup	250 mL
Chives, chopped	1/4 cup	60 mL
Sea salt, to taste		
Pepper, to taste		
Olive oil, for brushing	4 tsp.	20 mL
Kosher salt	2 tsp.	10 mL
Pepper, to taste		

Remove beef medallions from refrigerator 15 minutes before cooking.

To prepare mushrooms, heat olive oil in a frying pan on medium-high and cook shallots until soft. Add chanterelles and garlic and cook for 5 to 7 minutes. Add white wine and cook until liquid evaporates. Remove from heat and stir in parsley and chives. Season with salt and pepper.

Brush beef lightly with olive oil and season with salt and pepper. Place on grill and cook on medium-high, without moving it, until nice grill marks appear, about 4 minutes. Turn medallions and continue to grill until medium-rare, about 3 to 4 minutes more. Set aside on a cutting board to rest for 5 minutes before serving. Divide medallions among plates and spoon on mushrooms. Makes 4 servings.

1 serving: 390 Calories; 20 g Total Fat (10 g Mono, 1.5 g Poly, 6 g Sat); 85 mg Cholesterol; 8 g Carbohydrate (2 g Fibre, 3 g Sugar); 40 g Protein; 1240 mg Sodium

Italian Pot Roast

Good things come to those who wait. A long cooking time makes this recipe perfect for a relaxed weekend. There is plenty of tasty sauce to serve over pasta, potatoes or polenta.

Boneless beef blade (or chuck) roast	3 lbs.	1.4 kg
Salt	1/2 tsp.	2 mL
Pepper	1/4 tsp.	1 mL
Olive oil	2 tsp.	10 mL
Bacon slices, chopped	2	2
Chopped onion	1 1/2 cups	375 mL
Chopped celery	1 cup	250 mL
Dried oregano	1 tsp.	5 mL
Garlic cloves, minced	2	2
All-purpose flour	1/4 cup	60 mL
Prepared beef broth	2 cups	500 mL
Can of diced tomatoes, drained (28 oz., 796 mL)	1	1
Dry red wine	1 cup	250 mL
Bay leaves	2	2

Sprinkle roast with salt and pepper. Heat olive oil in a Dutch oven on medium-high. Add roast. Cook for about 10 minutes, turning occasionally, until browned on all sides. Transfer to a large plate. Reduce heat to medium.

Add bacon to same pot. Cook for about 3 minutes, stirring often, until almost crisp. Add next 4 ingredients. Cook for about 8 minutes, stirring often, until onion starts to soften.

Add flour. Cook, stirring, for 1 minute.

Slowly add broth, stirring constantly and scraping any brown bits from bottom of pot, until smooth. Stir in remaining 3 ingredients. Add roast. Cook, covered, in 300ºF (150ºC) oven for about 3 1/2 hours until roast is tender. Remove roast to a cutting board. Cover with foil and let stand for 10 minutes before slicing. Remove and discard bay leaves from sauce. Skim and discard fat. Serve sauce with roast. Makes 10 servings.

1 serving: 420 Calories; 28 g Total Fat (12 g Mono, 1.5 g Poly, 11 g Sat); 100 mg Cholesterol; 10 g Carbohydrate (1 g Fibre, 4 g Sugar); 26 g Protein; 650 mg Sodium

Slow Stroganoff Stew

Take it slow with this rich and decadent classic. Tender beef in a creamy red wine tomato sauce just shouldn't be rushed. Serve over egg noodles or rice.

All-purpose flour	3 tbsp.	45 mL
Stewing beef, cut into 1 inch (2.5 cm) pieces	2 lbs.	900 g
Cooking oil	2 tbsp.	30 mL
Cooking oil	2 tsp.	10 mL
Sliced fresh white mushrooms	1 1/2 cups	375 mL
Thinly sliced onion	1 1/2 cups	375 mL
Paprika	2 tsp.	10 mL
Can of diced tomatoes (with juice) (14 oz., 398 mL)	1	1
Dry red wine	1/2 cup	125 mL
Prepared beef broth	1/2 cup	125 mL
Tomato paste (see Tip, page 64)	3 tbsp.	45 mL
Granulated sugar	1/2 tsp.	2 mL
Salt	1/4 tsp.	1 mL
Pepper	1/4 tsp.	1 mL
Sour cream	1/3 cup	75 mL

Measure flour into a large resealable freezer bag. Add beef and toss until coated.

Heat first amount of cooking oil in large frying pan on medium. Add beef. Discard any remaining flour. Cook for 8 to 10 minutes, stirring occasionally, until browned. Transfer to 3 1/2 to 4 quart (3.5 to 4 L) slow cooker.

Heat second amount of cooking oil in same frying pan on medium. Add mushrooms and onion. Cook for 5 to 10 minutes, stirring occasionally and scraping any brown bits from bottom of pan, until onion is softened. Add paprika. Cook, stirring, for 1 minute. Add to slow cooker.

Stir in next 7 ingredients. Cook, covered, on Low for 9 to 10 hours or on High for 4 1/2 to 5 hours.

Stir in sour cream. Makes about 5 1/2 cups (1.4 L).

1 cup (250 mL): 425 Calories; 21 g Total Fat (9 g Mono, 2.5 g Poly, 7 g Sat); 85 mg Cholesterol; 14 g Carbohydrate (2 g Fibre, 6 g Sugar); 40 g Protein; 520 mg Sodium

Osso Buco

*This dish hails from Milan, where it is traditionally topped with gremolata
(a mixture of chopped parsley, garlic and lemon zest) and served over
a saffron risotto. Outside of Mlan, osso buco is often paired with polenta,
as it is in this photo.*

All-purpose flour	1 cup	250 mL
Salt	2 tsp.	10 mL
Pepper	1/2 tsp.	2 mL
Veal shanks, cut into 2 inch (5 cm) lengths	3	3
Cooking oil	1/4 cup	60 mL
Large onions, cut into wedges	3	3
Medium carrots, chopped	10	10
Sliced celery	1 1/2 cups	375 mL
Parsley flakes	1 tbsp.	15 mL
Dry white wine	1 cup	250 mL
Prepared beef broth	2 cups	500 mL
Cans of tomato sauce) (7 1/2 oz., 213 mL, each	2	2
Lemon juice	1 tbsp.	15 mL

Combine flour, salt and pepper in a plastic bag. Add veal, a few pieces at
a time, and shake to coat. Heat oil in a large frying pan on medium. Add
veal and sear until browned, adding more oil if necessary.

Combine onion, carrot, celery and parsley in a roaster. Place veal over
vegetables.

Add wine to frying pan and scrape any brown bits from bottom of pan.
Boil until liquid is reduced by a quarter.

Add broth, tomato sauce and lemon juice. Pour over contents in roaster.
Bake, covered, in 325ºF (160ºC) oven for about 2 hours until veal is fork
tender, adding more liquid if necessary. Gravy should be thick when done.
If too thin, remove veal and vegetables and boil sauce, uncovered, until
thickened. Makes 8 servings.

*1 serving: 360 Calories; 12 g Total Fat (6 g Mono, 2.5 g Poly, 2 g Sat); 95 mg Cholesterol;
30 g Carbohydrate (4 g Fibre, 9 g Sugar); 29 g Protein; 1210 mg Sodium*

Beef Bourguignon

This classic dish originated in the Burgundy region of France, an area known for its excellent wines. It pairs well with hot cooked noodles.

All-purpose flour	1/4 cup	60 mL
Salt	1/4 tsp.	1 mL
Pepper	1/4 tsp.	1 mL
Round blade or sirloin steak, cut into 3/4 inch (2 cm) cubes	2 lbs.	900 g
Dry red wine	2 cups	500 mL
Can of condensed beef consommé (10 oz., 284 mL)	1	1
Bay leaves	2	2
Vegetable oil	1 1/2 tsp.	7 mL
Garlic clove, minced	1	1
Sliced fresh mushrooms	2 cups	500 mL
Pepper, to taste		
Shallots, peeled	18	18
Diagonally sliced carrot	3 1/2 cups	875 mL
Chopped fresh parsley	1/4 cup	60 mL

Combine flour, salt and pepper in a plastic bag. Add beef cubes, a few at a time, and shake to coat. Place beef in a lightly sprayed roaster. Bake, uncovered, in 425ºF (220ºC) oven for 10 minutes or until browned, stirring once. Add wine, consommé and bay leaves. Bake, covered, in 350ºF (175ºC) oven for 2 1/2 hours.

Heat oil in a medium frying pan. Cook garlic, mushrooms and pepper until browned. Add to beef mixture.

Stir shallots, carrots and parsley into beef mixture. Cook, covered, for 1 hour until beef and vegetables are tender. Remove and discard bay leaves. Makes 6 servings.

1 serving: 390 Calories; 12 g Total Fat (6 g Mono, 1 g Poly, 4.5 g Sat); 80 mg Cholesterol; 22 g Carbohydrate (3 g Fibre, 6 g Sugar); 33 g Protein; 610 mg Sodium

Beef and Pears in Wine

Tender, flavourful beef complemented by a fruity wine sauce. To ensure even cooking, take the beef out the fridge 30 minutes before cooking. Serve with buttered pasta.

Beef tenderloin roast (1/2 to 3/4 lb., 225 to 340 g)	1	1
Cooking oil	1 tsp.	5 mL
Pepper, to taste		
Cooking oil	2 tsp.	10 mL
Diced onion	2 tbsp.	30 mL
Dry red wine	1 cup	250 mL
Redcurrant jelly	2 tbsp.	30 mL
Dijon mustard	2 tsp.	10 mL
Firm medium pear, peeled, cored and quartered	1	1

Drizzle roast with oil and sprinkle with pepper. Cook, uncovered, in 350°F (175°C) oven for 40 to 45 minutes until meat thermometer reads 140°F (60°C) for medium doneness or until desired doneness. Transfer to a cutting board. Tent with foil and let stand for 10 minutes.

Heat second amount of cooking oil in a medium saucepan on medium-low. Add onion and cook for 5 minutes, stirring occasionally, until onion is soft.

Stir in wine, jelly and mustard until jelly melts. Bring to a boil, then reduce heat to medium-low.

Add pear. Simmer, uncovered, for 10 to 15 minutes, stirring occasionally, until pear is soft. Remove pear and set aside, keeping it warm. Strain wine mixture, discarding solids. Return mixture to saucepan and boil, uncovered, on medium-high for about 5 minutes, stirring occasionally, until thickened. Drizzle over sliced beef and reserved pear. Makes 2 servings.

1 serving: 390 Calories; 15 g Total Fat (7 g Mono, 2 g Poly, 3.5 g Sat); 55 mg Cholesterol; 18 g Carbohydrate (3 g Fibre, 9 g Sugar); 24 g Protein; 130 mg Sodium

Braised Borscht Kabobs

A tasty reconstruction of a classic, with more tender pork than you can shake a stick at.

Butter	1 tbsp.	15 mL
Pork loin, cut into 1 inch (2.5 cm) cubes	1 lbs.	900 g
White wine	1 cup	250 mL
Apple juice	2 cups	500 mL
Water	2 cups	500 mL
Red cabbage, quatered, inner leaves removed	1/2	1/2
Ground cinnamon	1/2 tsp.	2 mL
Fennel seed	1/4 tsp.	1 mL
Ground cloves	1/4 tsp.	1 mL
Lemon juice	2 tbsp.	30 mL
Salt	1/2 tsp.	2 mL
Red beets, cut in 1 inch (2.5 cm) chunks	4	4
Leeks (white part only), cut into 1 inch (2.5 cm) chunks	5	5
Carrots, cut into 1 inch (2.5 cm) chunks	5	5
Sour cream	1/4 cup	60 mL
Dill, chopped	2 tsp.	10 mL

Heat butter in a large heavy bottomed, oven-safe pan over medium-high. Add pork and sear until golden brown on all sides.

Pour in 1/2 cup (125 L) wine to deglaze pan, then add remaining wine, apple juice and water. Break apart cabbage leaves and mix next 8 ingredients, ensuring meat and vegetables are submerged in liquid. Add more water if necessary. Cook in 350ºF (175ºC) oven for 2 hours, or until pork chunks can be cut with a fork. Remove pan from oven and allow to rest for 15 minutes. Strain liquid into a heavy bottomed pot and cook on high until volume is reduced by three-quarters and liquid has reached a syrupy consistency.

Thread pork and vegetables evenly on 8 inch (20 cm) skewers. Generously brush kabobs with syrupy liquid and cook in 450ºF (230ºC) oven for 5 minutes to glaze. Remove from oven and let stand for 4 minutes.

Combine sour cream and dill and transfer to a fine-tip squeeze bottle. Squeeze sour cream mixture over top of each kabob and serve. Makes 10 skewers.

1 skewer: *270 Calories; 8 g Total Fat (3 g Mono, 1 g Poly, 3.5 g Sat); 65 mg Cholesterol; 25 g Carbohydrate (4 g Fibre, 14 g Sugar); 21 g Protein; 260 mg Sodium*

Wine-sauced Pork Fettuccine

Notes of wine, garlic and cheese provide a lovely accompaniment for tender pork sausage and pasta. A dish that's sure to have broad appeal. Garish with cherry tomatoes and fresh greens for a lovely presentation.

Fettuccine	8 oz.	225 g
Olive oil	1 tbsp.	15 mL
Italian sausage, casings removed	1 lb.	454 g
Olive oil	1 tsp.	5 mL
Chopped onion	1 cup	250 mL
Dijon mustard	1 tbsp.	15 mL
Garlic cloves, minced	3	3
Dry white wine	1/2 cup	125 mL
Prepared chicken broth	1 cup	250 mL
Chopped fresh parsley	1/4 cup	60 mL
Grated Romano cheese	1/4 cup	60 mL

Cook pasta according to package directions. Drain. Return to same pot. Cover to keep warm.

Heat first amount of olive oil in large frying pan on medium-high. Add pork. Cook for about 2 minutes, crumbling with spoon, until no pink remains. Remove to a large plate. Cover to keep warm. Reduce heat to medium.

Heat second amount of olive oil in same frying pan. Add onion. Cook for about 5 minutes, stirring often, until softened. Add mustard and garlic. Cook, stirring, for about 1 minute until fragrant.

Add wine. Cook, stirring, for 2 minutes. Stir in broth and parsley and bring to a boil. Add pork and reduce heat to medium-low. Cook, stirring, for about 2 minutes until heated through. Add to pasta.

Sprinkle with cheese and toss. Makes about 8 cups (2 L).

1 cup (250 mL): 360 Calories; 21 g Total Fat (10 g Mono, 2.5 g Poly, 7 g Sat); 45 mg Cholesterol; 25 g Carbohydrate (trace Fibre, 13 g Sugar); 18 g Protein; 550 mg Sodium

Port Wine Chops with Figs

Gather around the table for sophisticated yet family-friendly flavours—pepper-speckled pork chops with a sweet port and fig glaze. Serve these richly flavoured chops with rice pilaf and a salad.

Bone-in pork chops, trimmed of fat	6	6
Salt	1/2 tsp.	5 mL
Coarsely ground pepper	1 tsp.	5 mL
Cooking oil	1 tbsp.	15 mL
Cooking oil	1 tsp.	5 mL
Diced red onion	2 tbsp.	30 mL
Port wine	1 cup	250 mL
Red wine vinegar	1/4 cup	60 mL
Dried figs, quartered	12	12
Chopped fresh rosemary	3/4 tsp.	4 mL
Half-and-half cream	3 tbsp.	45 mL
Cornstarch	1/2 tsp.	2 mL

Sprinkle both sides of chops with salt and pepper. Heat first amount of cooking oil in a large frying pan on medium. Cook chops, in 2 batches, for about 5 minutes per side until no longer pink inside. Transfer to a serving platter and tent with foil.

Add second amount of cooking oil to same frying pan. Add onion and cook for about 2 minutes, stirring often, until softened.

Stir in next 4 ingredients. Boil gently, uncovered, for about 5 minutes until liquid is reduced by half.

Stir cream into cornstarch in a small cup until smooth. Add to fig mixture. Heat, stirring, for about 1 minute until boiling and thickened. Serve with pork chops. Makes 6 servings.

1 serving: 350 Calories; 17 g Total Fat (8 g Mono, 2.5 g Poly, 5 g Sat); 65 mg Cholesterol; 18 g Carbohydrate (2 g Fibre, 12 g Sugar); 21 g Protein; 250 mg Sodium

Lamb and Red Wine Braise

Elegant and delicious, this dish is sophisticated enough to please the most discerning dinner guest while still being family friendly. You can use stewing beef in place of the lamb if you prefer.

All-purpose flour	1/4 cup	60 mL
Lamb stewing meat (such as leg or shoulder), cut into 3/4 inch (2 cm) pieces	4 lbs.	1.8 kg
Olive oil	2 tbsp.	30 mL
Olive oil	1 tbsp.	15 mL
Coarsely chopped carrot	1 1/2 cups	375 mL
Coarsely chopped onion	1 1/2 cups	375 mL
Sliced mushrooms	2 cups	500 mL
Garlic cloves, minced	4	4
Red wine	1 1/2 cups	375 mL
Prepared chicken broth	1 cup	250 mL
Tomato paste	1/4 cup	60 mL
Sprigs of fresh rosemary	4	4
Salt	1/2 tsp.	2 mL
Pepper	1/2 tsp.	2 mL

Toss flour and lamb in batches in a large plastic bag until lamb is coated. Heat first amount of olive oil in a large pot on medium-high. Add lamb in batches and sear until browned, adding more oil if necessary. Remove lamb from pot.

Heat second amount of oil in pot on medium. Add carrot and onion and cook, stirring often, for about 5 minutes until onion is softened. Add mushrooms and garlic and cook for about 5 minutes until mushrooms are softened.

Stir in lamb and remaining 6 ingredients. Bring to a boil, then reduce heat to low. Cook, covered, for 1 hour, stirring occasionally, until lamb is tender and sauce is thickened. Makes 8 servings.

1 serving: 440 Calories; 17 g Total Fat (9 g Mono, 1.5 g Poly, 5 g Sat); 145 mg Cholesterol; 12 g Carbohydrate (2 g Fibre, 4 g Sugar); 48 g Protein; 410 mg Sodium

Cioppino with Fennel and Saffron

Cioppino is an Italian seafood stew whose North American roots are thought to have originated in the San Francisco Bay area when Italian immigrants from Genoa replaced traditional Genoese ingredients with the fresh fish available to them on the West Coast. It is traditional to serve cioppino with polenta and a bottle of Chianti.

Snapper fillet, cleaned	2 lbs.	900 g
Fresh shrimp, tails on	1 lb.	454 g
Clams, mussels and scallops	1/2 lb.	225 g
Mussels (see Tip, page 64)	1/2 lb.	225 g
Scallops	1/2 lb.	225 g
Crab, cooked, cleaned and cracked	1	1
Extra virgin olive oil	2 tbsp.	30 mL
Small onion, minced	1	1
Medium fennel bulb, diced	1	1
White wine	1 cup	250 mL
Garlic cloves, minced	3	3
Zest from half an orange, minced		
Pinch of saffron, or to taste, dissolved in 1/4 cup (60 mL) warm stock		
Tomato sauce	4 cups	1 L
Fish stock	3 cups	750 mL
Sea salt, to taste		
Pepper, to taste		
Fresh basil	1/2 cup	125 mL

Wash all fish and seafood, except crab, and pat dry. Heat oil in a heavy-bottomed pot and sauté onion. Stir in fennel and sauté for 5 minutes.

Add wine and garlic, and simmer for 10 minutes. Stir in orange zest, saffron, tomato sauce and stock, and simmer for 10 minutes. Nestle fish fillets and seafood into sauce, making sure to cover them with liquid. Cover, bring back to a simmer on medium-high and cook until clams and mussels open, about 10 to 12 minutes. Season with salt and pepper. Serve hot in warmed bowls, garnished with fresh basil. Makes 6 servings.

1 serving: 520 Calories; 11 g Total Fat (4.5 g Mono, 2.5 g Poly, 2 g Sat); 230 mg Cholesterol; 18 g Carbohydrate (3 g Fibre, 6 g Sugar); 75 g Protein; 2050 mg Sodium

Spaghetti Arcobaleno

This dish features an attractive arcobaleno (Italian for "rainbow") of fresh ingredients in a delicious light sauce. Garnish with shaved Parmesan cheese and small basil leaves.

Spaghetti	8 oz.	225 g
Olive oil	1 tsp.	5 mL
Salmon fillets, skin and any small bones removed	1 lb.	454 g
Halved grape tomatoes	2 cups	500 mL
Chopped yellow pepper	1 1/2 cups	375 mL
Whole pitted kalamata olives	1 cup	250 mL
Dry white wine	1/2 cup	125 mL
Sun-dried tomato pesto	1/2 cup	125 mL
Salt	1/4 tsp.	1 mL
Chopped fresh asparagus (1 inch, 2.5 cm, pieces)	2 cups	500 mL
Coarsely chopped fresh basil (or 2 tbsp., 30 mL, dried)	1/2 cup	125 mL
Lemon juice	1 tbsp.	30 mL
Grated lemon zest (see Tip, page 64)	1 tsp.	5 mL
Pepper	1/4 tsp.	1 mL

Cook pasta according to package directions. Drain and set aside. Heat olive oil in a large frying pan on medium. Add fillets. Cook for about 4 minutes per side until fish flakes easily when tested with a fork. Transfer to a plate. Cover to keep warm.

Add next 6 ingredients to same frying pan. Bring to a boil. Cook for about 10 minutes, stirring occasionally, until yellow pepper is tender.

Stir in asparagus and pasta. Cook, covered, for about 1 minute until asparagus is tender-crisp. Transfer to a large serving bowl. Break up salmon pieces. Add to pasta mixture.

Toss in remaining 4 ingredients. Makes about 8 1/2 cups (2.1 L).

1 cup (250 mL): 290 Calories; 12 g Total Fat (4 g Mono, 1.5 g Poly, 1.5 g Sat); 30 mg Cholesterol; 27 g Carbohydrate (3 g Fibre, 3 g Sugar); 16 g Protein; 449 mg Sodium

Mussels with White Wine and Garlic

Simple and delicious. Soak up the tasty sauce with fresh crusty bread or toast.

Mussels (see Tip, page 64)	4 lbs.	1.8 kg
White wine such as Chardonnay	1 cup	250 mL
Garlic cloves, minced	4	4
Butter	1 tbsp.	15 mL
Chopped chives	1/4 cup	60 mL

Scrub mussels under cool running water and remove any beards. Discard mussels that don't close when gently tapped.

Place white wine and garlic in a large pot and bring to a boil. Add mussels to pot, cover and reduce heat, cooking for about 5 to 6 minutes. Discard any mussels that have not opened. With a slotted spoon transfer mussels to serving dishes.

Turn heat to high and bring remaining liquid to a boil. Cook for 2 to 3 minutes, until it has reduced slightly, and whisk in butter. Spoon sauce over mussels, sprinkle with chives and serve hot. Makes 5 servings.

1 serving: 380 Calories; 10 g Total Fat (2.5 g Mono, 2.5 g Poly, 3 g Sat); 110 mg Cholesterol; 16 g Carbohydrate (0 g Fibre, trace Sugar); 43 g Protein; 1060 mg Sodium

Chili Wine Seafood Linguini

Not your average cream sauce! We've spiked this seafood-laden pasta with wine and jalapeños for a spicy bite you won't soon forget.

Linguine	12 oz.	340 g
Olive oil	1 tsp.	5 mL
Finely chopped prosciutto	1/3 cup	75 mL
Garlic cloves, minced	2	2
Half-and-half cream	2 cups	500 mL
Dry white wine	1/2 cup	125 mL
Butter	2 tbsp.	30 mL
Finely chopped jalapeño pepper, drained	1 tbsp.	15 mL
Salt	1/2 tsp.	2 mL
Pepper	1/4 tsp.	1 mL
Small bay scallops	1/2 lb.	225 g
Uncooked medium shrimp (peeled and deveined)	1/2 lb.	225 g
Lemon juice	1 tbsp.	15 mL
Chopped fresh parsley	1 tbsp.	15 mL

Cook linguini according to package directions and set aside, keeping it warm.

Heat olive oil in a large frying an on medium. Add prosciutto and garlic. Cook, stirring, for about 2 minutes until fragrant.

Stir in next 6 ingredients. Simmer, uncovered, for 8 to 10 minutes, stirring occasionally, until slightly thickened.

Stir in scallops and shrimp. Cook for 3 to 5 minutes until shrimp turn pink and scallops are opaque. Remove from heat.

Stir in lemon juice. Add to pasta and toss until coated. Sprinkle with parsley. Makes 4 servings.

1 serving: 690 Calories; 27 g Total Fat (6 g Mono, 1 g Poly, 14 g Sat); 110 mg Cholesterol; 73 g Carbohydrate (2 g Fibre, 4 g Sugar); 34 g Protein; 1050 mg Sodium

Poached Trout with Salsa Rouge

In this relatively low-fat dish, softly poached trout is paired with a sweet pepper salsa. Serve with fresh mixed greens.

Balsamic vinegar	1/2 cup	125 mL
Honey	1 tbsp.	15 mL
White wine	2 cups	500 mL
Lemon juice	3 tbsp.	45 mL
Lemon zest	1 tbsp.	15 mL
Salt	1/4 tsp.	1 mL
Saffron threads (optional)	7	7
Vegetable broth or water	4 cups	1 L
Pine nuts	1/2 cup	125 mL
Chopped fresh parsley	2 tbsp.	30 mL
Roasted red peppers	1/4 cup	60 mL
Smoked (sweet) paprika	1/2 tsp.	2 mL
Cayenne pepper	1/8 tsp.	0.5 mL
Grainy Dijon mustard	1 tsp.	5 mL
Ground cloves	1/8 tsp.	0.5 mL
Melted butter	2 tbsp.	30 mL
Fresh trout fillets	6	6

Pour vinegar into a small saucepan and cook on medium heat until reduced by half and a syrupy consistency. Stir in honey and transfer to a small squeeze bottle.

Combine next 6 ingredients in a medium pot and bring to a boil.

To make salsa, place pine nuts in a food processor or blender and pulse until chunky. Blend in next 6 ingredients. Gradually pour in melted butter. Transfer to a small bowl and set aside.

Lay trout fillets flat in a roasting pan, ensuring they do not overlap. Pour boiling liquid over trout so fillets are fully submerged. If more liquid is needed, add hot tap water. Bake in 375ºF (175ºC) oven for 11 to 13 minutes, or until fish is just firm. Remove from oven and leave trout in liquid to rest for 4 minutes. To serve, spoon salsa over each fillet and drizzle with balsamic reduction. Makes 6 servings.

1 serving: 460 Calories; 23 g Total Fat (9 g Mono, 7 g Poly, 4.5 g Sat); 110 mg Cholesterol; 11 g Carbohydrate (trace Fibre, 7 g Sugar); 38 g Protein; 260 mg Sodium

Pacific Scallops with Double Smoked Bacon and Vanilla

Pacific scallops are always a treat (when you can get them), but when paired with double smoked bacon and a hint of vanilla, they are incredible. Serve with fresh greens.

Diced double smoked bacon	2/3 cup	150 mL
Minced shallots	2 tbsp.	30 mL
Dry sparkling wine	1 cup	250 mL
Vanilla bean pod	1/2	1/2
Champagne vinegar	1/2 tsp.	2 mL
Cold unsalted butter, cut into small pieces	1 cup	250 mL
Sea salt, to taste		
White pepper, to taste		
Olive oil	1 tbsp.	15 mL
Pacific scallops	12	12
Sea salt, to taste		
Pepper, to taste		

In a medium saucepan, sauté bacon until crispy. Set bacon aside and stir in shallots, sparkling wine, vanilla bean pod and seeds (see Tip, page 64), and bring to a boil. Reduce heat to medium-low and simmer until you have about 1/4 cup (60 mL) of liquid remaining.

Stir in champagne vinegar and remove vanilla pod. Turn heat down to very low and, little by little, whisk in butter, 1 piece at a time. When sauce will coat back of a spoon, stir in bacon and season sauce with salt and pepper. Keep sauce warm but off direct heat until ready to serve.

Heat olive oil in a large pan on medium-high. Season scallops on all sides with salt and pepper. Sear for 2 to 3 minutes until nicely caramelized. Turn scallops over and cook for an additional 3 minutes. Serve immediately with sauce. Makes 4 servings.

1 serving: 850 Calories; 80 g Total Fat (28 g Mono, 6 g Poly, 40 g Sat); 180 mg Cholesterol; 6 g Carbohydrate (0 g Fibre, 1 g Sugar); 16 g Protein; 700 mg Sodium

Mushroom Cap Artichokes

Warm, creamy cheese with a smack of spice and artichoke in a mushroom head that has been braised in white wine. Sophisticated yet family friendly fare that will have even the youngsters clamouring for more.

Allowing the mushrooms to rest after they have been broiled both in the liquid and again with the cheese mixture makes a real difference in the overall quality of this dish. It's worth your time to just let them sit.

White mushrooms	20	20
White wine	3 cups	750 mL
Diced fresh thyme	1 tbsp.	15 mL
Light cream cheese	8 oz.	250 g
Smoked Gouda, grated	2 oz.	57 g
Small green jalapeño, finely diced	1	1
Canned artichoke hearts, chopped	1/4 cup	60 mL
Garlic cloves, finely diced	2	2
Flaxseed	2 tsp.	10 mL

De-stem mushrooms and remove gills with a small spoon. Arrange upside down on a medium-sized roasting pan—mushrooms should fit snugly together. Pour wine over mushrooms, ensuring they are fully submerged, and sprinkle thyme over top. Add water if you need more liquid to cover mushrooms. Bake in 375°F (190°C) oven for 25 minutes. Remove from oven and allow mushrooms to cool in their liquid.

Whip cream cheese and Gouda together until fluffy. Fold in jalapeño, artichoke, garlic and flaxseed. Remove mushrooms from liquid and transfer to a baking sheet. Generously spoon cheese mixture into mushrooms. Broil on high heat for 5 minutes or until cheese begins to brown slightly. Remove from oven and allow to cool for 5 minutes. Serve warm. Makes 20 mushroom caps.

1 mushroom cap: 70 Calories; 3.5 g Total Fat (0 g Mono, 0 g Poly, 2 g Sat); 10 mg Cholesterol; 3 g Carbohydrate (0 g Fibre, 2 g Sugar); 2 g Protein; 105 mg Sodium

Gnocchi in a Sorrel Sauce

Gnocchi, which means "dumplings" in Italian, are one of the most versatile Italian dishes. The secret to gnocchi is to not overcook them because they will start to fall apart. As with all Italian pasta dishes, al dente, or "tender to the tooth," is the desired doneness.

Package of gnocchi (1 lb., 500 g)	1	1
Olive oil	1 tbsp.	15 mL
Unsalted butter	1 tbsp.	15 mL
Small shallot, minced	1	1
White wine	1/2 cup	125 mL
Heavy cream (32%)	1 cup	250 mL
Sorrel, chopped	1 cup	250 mL
Chopped parsley	1/4 cup	60 mL
Sea salt, to taste		
Pepper, to taste		
Chopped fresh chives, as a garnish		
Freshly grated Parmesan cheese, as a garnish		

Bring a big pot of salted water to a rolling boil and cook gnocchi until they float to surface. Drain, toss with olive oil and set aside.

Heat butter in a large saucepan on medium-high. Add shallot and cook for 2 to 3 minutes. Add wine and cook until wine has reduced by half. Add cream and cook for 5 minutes.

Purée sorrel and parsley in a blender along with hot cream mixture until everything is incorporated; sauce will turn a jade green colour. Pour sauce back into pan along with gnocchi to heat through and season with salt and pepper. Serve in warm bowls garnished with chives and Parmesan cheese. Makes 2 servings.

1 serving: 850 Calories; 37 g Total Fat (13 g Mono, 2 g Poly, 19 g Sat); 135 mg Cholesterol; 102 g Carbohydrate (7 g Fibre, 4 g Sugar); 17 g Protein; 1180 mg Sodium

Wild Rice and Lentil Pilaf

A light summer dish with Indian spices and sweet mango. Rich in folate, thiamin, protein and dietary fibre.

Butter	2 tbsp.	30 mL
Mushrooms, finely diced	1 cup	250 mL
White wine	1 cup	250 mL
Garlic cloves, minced	3	3
Chopped dried mango	1/8 cup	30 mL
Coriander	1/4 tsp.	1 mL
Cumin	1/8 tsp.	0.5 mL
Green lentils	3/4 cup	175 mL
Wild rice or whole grain rice	1 1/2 cups	325 mL
Vegetable broth	6 cups	1.5 mL
White onion	1/2	1/2
Bay leaves	2	2
Chopped almonds	1/8 cup	30 mL
Chopped cilantro	1 tbsp.	15 mL

Preheat oven to 350ºF (175ºC). Melt butter in a large heavy-bottomed pan on medium-high. Cook mushrooms until they are browned. Pour in wine and reduce by three-quarters. Lower heat and add garlic, mango, coriander, cumin, lentils and rice. Cook for an additional 3 minutes on low heat to allow flavours to blend.

Transfer to a medium casserole dish and pour broth over rice mixture. Stir in onion and bay leaves. Cook, covered, in 350ºF (175ºC) oven for 60 to 75 minutes or until lentils and rice are tender. Remove from oven and discard onion and bay leaves. Fluff with a fork, garnish with almonds and cilantro and serve. Makes 6 servings.

1 serving: 330 Calories; 6 g Total Fat (2 g Mono, 0.5 g Poly, 2.5 g Sat); 10 mg Cholesterol; 52 g Carbohydrate (7 g Fibre, 6 g Sugar); 12 g Protein; 600 mg Sodium

Eggplant Parmigiana

This slimmed-down version is much lower in fat and sodium than the traditional version with breaded, fried eggplant. Serve with a leafy green salad and crusty bread.

Can of diced tomatoes (with juice) (28 oz., 796 mL)	1	1
Dry white wine	1/2 cup	125 mL
Tomato paste (see Tip, page 64)	3 tbsp.	45 mL
Dried basil	1 1/2 tsp.	7 mL
Dried oregano	1 1/2 tsp.	7 mL
Garlic cloves, minced	2	2
Medium eggplants (with peel), about 1 1/4 lbs. (560 g) each	2	2
Salt, to taste		
Pepper, to taste		
Grated Italian cheese blend	1 1/3 cups	325 mL
Grated Parmesan cheese	1/4 cup	60 mL

Process first 6 ingredients in blender or food processor until smooth.

Slice eggplants crosswise, about 1/4 inch (6 mm) thick. Discard outer slices. Arrange in a single layer on greased baking sheets with sides. Sprinkle both sides with salt and pepper. Broil on centre rack in oven for about 8 minutes per side until browned and softened.

To assemble, layer ingredients in a greased 9 x 13 inch (23 x 33 cm) baking dish as follows: 1/3 of tomato mixture; half of eggplant slices, overlapping if necessary; half of Italian cheese blend; 1/3 of tomato mixture; remaining eggplant slices, overlapping if necessary; remaining tomato mixture; remaining Italian cheese blend. Sprinkle with Parmesan cheese. Bake, uncovered, in 350°F (175°C) oven for about 45 minutes until cheese is golden. Let stand for 10 minutes. Cuts into 6 pieces.

1 piece: 170 Calories; 6 g Total Fat (0 g Mono, 0 g Poly, 0 g Sat); 20 mg Cholesterol; 19 g Carbohydrate (7 g Fibre, 10 g Sugar); 10 g Protein; 680 mg Sodium

Butternut Pesto Risotto

The butternut squash breaks down a bit as the risotto cooks, lending this dish a lovely golden colour.

Prepared vegetable broth	4 cups	1 L
Olive oil	1 tsp.	5 mL
Chopped celery	1 cup	250 mL
Chopped onion	1 cup	250 mL
Pepper	1/4 tsp.	1 mL
Garlic cloves, minced	2	2
Diced butternut squash (see Tip, page 64)	2 cup	500 mL
Arborio rice	1 cup	250 mL
Dry white wine	1/2 cup	125 mL
Diced red pepper	1 cup	250 mL
Grated Parmesan cheese	1/2 cup	125 mL
Basil pesto	2 tbsp.	30 mL
Pine nuts, toasted	2 tbsp.	30 mL
Chopped fresh parsley	1 tbsp.	15 mL
Lemon juice	1 tbsp.	15 mL

Bring broth to a boil in small saucepan. Reduce heat to low. Cover to keep warm.

Heat olive oil in a large saucepan on medium. Add next 4 ingredients. Cook for about 8 minutes, stirring often, until celery is softened.

Add squash and rice. Cook, stirring, for 1 minute. Stir in wine and cook, stirring, for about 1 minute until liquid is evaporated. Add 1 cup (250 mL) hot broth, stirring constantly until broth is almost absorbed. Repeat 2 more times, adding broth 1 cup (250 mL) at a time. Add red pepper and remaining cup of broth, stirring constantly until broth is absorbed and rice is tender and creamy.

Stir in remaining 5 ingredients. Makes about 5 2/3 cups (1.4 L).

1 cup (250 mL): 260 Calories; 8 g Total Fat (2 g Mono, 1.5 g Poly, 2.5 g Sat); 10 mg Cholesterol; 40 g Carbohydrate (3 g Fibre, 6 g Sugar); 8 g Protein; 600 mg Sodium

Mushroom Ragout

This ragout is a perfect side for any grilled meat. You can use any mushrooms in this recipe. If you can get fresh wild mushrooms, that's great, but button mushrooms will work as well. Sometimes grocery stores will stock wild mushrooms, or you can check out the local farmers' markets. Morels usually appear in markets in spring, and throughout the summer different varieties are available across the country.

Extra-virgin olive oil	2 tbsp.	30 mL
Crushed red chili flakes	1 tsp.	5 mL
Garlic cloves, peeled	3	3
Onion, sliced	1/2	1/2
Mushrooms	2 lbs.	900 g
White wine	1/2 cup	125 mL
Tomatoes, diced	4	4
Balsamic vinegar	2 tbsp.	30 mL
Chopped fresh herbs (oregano, thyme, rosemary or a combination)	2 tbsp.	30 mL

Heat olive oil in a large skillet or Dutch oven on medium. Add red chili flakes and cook until they begin to crackle.

Add garlic and cook until golden brown.

Add onion and cook for 3 to 5 minutes or until soft.

Add mushrooms and cook for 3 to 5 minutes. Add remaining ingredients and turn heat to medium-low. Gently simmer, stirring occasionally, for up to 45 minutes. When most of the liquid has been reduced, taste and adjust seasonings. Makes 5 servings as a side.

1 serving: 130 Calories; 6 g Total Fat (4.5 g Mono, 1 g Poly, 1 g Sat); 0 mg Cholesterol; 12 g Carbohydrate (3 g Fibre, 6 g Sugar); 6 g Protein; 15 mg Sodium

Fruit Zabaglione

Zabaglione (pronounced zah-bahl-YOH-nay) is a warm, creamy custard typically made from egg yolks, wine and sugar. This mildly cinnamon-spiced version is guaranteed to live up to all expectations. Experiment with any combination of your favourite fresh fruit

Cherries	**3 cups**	**750 mL**
Egg yolks (large)	**4**	**4**
Marsala wine	**1/2 cup**	**125 mL**
Granulated sugar	**1/4 cup**	**60 mL**
Ground cinnamon, sprinkle		

Spoon cherries into 4 serving bowls.

Whisk remaining 4 ingredients in a medium heatproof bowl. Set bowl over simmering water in a large saucepan so that bottom of bowl is not touching water. Cook for about 7 minutes, whisking constantly, until foamy and thickened. Spoon over fruit. Makes 4 servings.

***1 serving:** 190 Calories; 4.5 g Total Fat (2 g Mono, 1 g Poly, 1.5 g Sat); 210 mg Cholesterol; 28 g Carbohydrate (2 g Fibre, 25 g Sugar); 4 g Protein; 10 mg Sodium*

Ginger-poached Pears

Ultra-sweet icewine is the perfect ingredient for poaching pears. Paired with ginger and lemon, it's one hot ticket to a higher level of taste. If you prefer red wine, feel free to substitute merlot for the icewine.

Small, firm peeled pears	4	4
Water	3 cups	750 mL
Icewine	1 cup	250 mL
Granulated sugar	1/2 cup	125 mL
Lemon juice	2 tbsp.	30 mL
Piece of gingerroot (1 inch, 2.5 cm, length), chopped	1	1

Core pears from the bottom, leaving stems intact. Cut a thin slice from bottoms so pears will stand upright.

Combine remaining 5 ingredients in a large saucepan. Bring to a boil, stirring to dissolve sugar. Reduce heat to medium-low. Lay pears on their sides in pan. Simmer, covered, for 20 to 25 minutes, turning occasionally, until pears are tender when pierced with a knife. Transfer pears to a serving dish, using a slotted spoon. Remove and discard ginger. Boil poaching liquid on medium-high for about 20 minutes until reduced and slightly thickened. Serve with pears. Makes 4 servings.

1 serving: 250 Calories; 0 g Total Fat (0 g Mono, 0 g Poly, 0 g Sat); 0 mg Cholesterol; 52 g Carbohydrate (5 g Fibre, 41 g Sugar); trace Protein; 5 mg Sodium

recipe index

topical tips

Fresh mussels: Use your fresh mussels within 24 hours of purchasing them. The best way to store fresh mussels is to put them in a colander and place the colander into a bowl. Cover the mussels with ice and then with a damp towel. The mussels will stay very cold and have good air circulation, without being submerged (or drowned) in water.

Handling squash: Some people have an allergic reaction to raw squash, so wear rubber gloves when handling raw butternut or acorn squash.

Tomato paste: If a recipe calls for less than an entire can of tomato paste, freeze the unopened can for 30 minutes. Open both ends and push the contents through one end. Slice off only what you need and freeze the remaining paste in a resealable freezer bag or plastic wrap for future use.

Vanilla pod: To get the most flavour out of a vanilla bean pod, carefully slice it open and scrape out the tiny seeds; use both seeds and pod in the recipe.

Zest first, juice second: When a recipe calls for grated zest and juice, it's easier to grate the fruit first, then juice it. Be careful not to grate down to the pith (white part of the peel), which is bitter and best avoided.

Nutrition Information Guidelines

Each recipe is analyzed using the Canadian Nutrient File from Health Canada, which is based on the United States Department of Agriculture (USDA) Nutrient Database.

- If more than one ingredient is listed (such as "butter or hard margarine"), or if a range is given (1–2 tsp., 5–10 mL), only the first ingredient or first amount is analyzed.

- For meat, poultry and fish, the serving size per person is based on the recommended 4 oz. (113 g) uncooked weight (without bone), which is 2–3 oz. (57–85 g) cooked weight (without bone)— approximately the size of a deck of playing cards.

- Milk used is 1% M.F. (milk fat), unless otherwise stated.

- Cooking oil used is canola oil, unless otherwise stated.

- Ingredients indicating "sprinkle," "optional" or "for garnish" are not included in the nutrition information.

- The fat in recipes and combination foods can vary greatly depending on the sources and types of fats used in each specific ingredient. For these reasons, the count of saturated, monounsaturated and polyunsaturated fats may not add up to the total fat content.